FIGHTING
BLIND

Basic Study of Spirit Warfare

Ronald W. Brisbee

ISBN 979-8-89485-642-1 (Paperback)
ISBN 979-8-89485-643-8 (Digital)

Covenant Books
11661 Hwy 707
Murrells Inlet, SC 29576
www.covenantbooks.com

IN THE BEGINNING

"In the beginning" is the first statement of God's Holy Word given to us. As we read through His Word, we find that the beginning of His creation as we know it and experience through our physical five senses is not the only creation of the Almighty God. There are many others. There are beginnings.

> For by him were all things created, that are in heaven, and that are in earth, visible and invisible, whether they be thrones, or dominions, or principalities, or powers: all things were created by him, and for him: And he is before all things, and by him all things consist. (Colossians 1:16–17)

> Thou, even thou, art LORD alone; thou hast made heaven, the heaven of heavens, with all their host, the earth, and all things that are therein, the

seas, and all that is therein, and
thou preservest them all; and the
host of heaven worshippeth thee.
(Nehemiah 9:6)

The natural question we have concerning them is, "When did they occur?" We are not given a definitive timeline or sequence other than the six days of God creating mankind, the heavens, and the earth as we know it, as described in Genesis chapter 1. There is much curiosity and debate as to exactly when God created the angels and the other "hosts of heaven." I am fairly confident that He is not done creating and has plans for many more wondrous marvels.

There are hosts of heaven other than angels named and described in the Holy Bible. A couple others were specifically named and described and where to find them in scripture: Cherubim in Genesis 3:24 and Seraphim in Isaiah 6:2. Without any doubt, the most well-known host of heaven created by God was Lucifer, who was later renamed Satan, and he was a cherub (Ezekiel 28:14; Isaiah 14:12–13). Satan rebelled against God, his creator, and was cast from heaven.

And he (Jesus) said unto
them, I beheld Satan as lightning
fall from heaven. (Luke 10:18)

When Satan fell from heaven, he was not alone. It is a common belief that one-third of the angels in heaven were cast down with Satan. Revelation 12:7–10 supports this belief. Those heavenly hosts that fell from heaven with Satan are now wandering the earth, and we know them today as demons, evil spirits, or unclean spirits. They are followers of and worship Satan.

We know that the fall of Satan from heaven took place before the creation described in Genesis chapter 1. Satan appears in the garden of Eden to tempt Eve in Genesis 3:1–14. After looking at a few other facts and considerations, we will come back to this point.

GOD KNOWS
ALL THINGS

Almighty God knows all, sees all, and hears all, and He is omnipresent, meaning that He is everywhere at once. You can find those facts in the following scriptures: Psalm 113:4–6, Psalm 139:7–10, Proverbs 15:3, Isaiah 57:15, Jeremiah 23:23–24. God knows all things (1 John 3:20, Isaiah 40:28, Hebrews 4:13).

> *Am* I a God at hand, saith the LORD, and not a God afar off? Can any hide himself in secret places that I shall not see him? Saith the LORD. Do not I fill heaven and earth? saith the LORD. (Jeremiah 23:23–24; emphasis mine)

Knowing that God knows all, sees all, hears all, and is omnipresent, the question arises: Where was God when Satan approached Eve in the garden of Eden and tempted her? He, God, was present. Satan and Eve were not alone. God was watching and listening, and He knew what the outcome would be. We obviously want to know, why would Almighty God the Father, our creator, stand back and allow it to happen?

The obvious answer is that this creation of God's is not all about us. It is critical that we understand this. When Satan fell from heaven as lightning, he fell to earth. And as described in Genesis 1:2, earth was without form and void. God created mankind in the dominion of Satan after Satan's fall from grace. Satan does not have authority over earth, but he is allowed dominion and influence.

> *And* we know that we are
> of God, and the whole world
> lieth in wickedness. (1 John 5:19;
> emphasis mine)

God granting access and allowing Satan to spend uninterrupted time tempting and deceiving Eve in Genesis chapter 3:1–14 shows us obviously that we are third parties and in the middle. The middle of what? Spirit warfare, to put it bluntly. There is so much more to God's purpose of this creation than we can imagine in our finite minds. We as humans like to think that it's all about us. We are by nature self-serving, selfish, and self-centered, but God created us, and He did not create us to make us happy.

God created us to make HIM happy and accomplish His plans in a spiritual realm rather than physical.

> For the creature was made subject to vanity, not willingly, but by reason of him who hath subjected *the same* in hope. (Romans 8:20; emphasis mine)

> As it is written, For thy sake we are killed all the day long; we are accounted as sheep for the slaughter. (Romans 8:36)

Why would He do that? His way of thinking is far above ours. To make sense of and understand His ultimate purpose is impossible for us. He even plainly tells us that in Isaiah 55:8–11.

> For my thoughts are not your thoughts, neither are your ways my ways, saith the LORD. For as the heavens are higher than the earth, so are my ways higher than your ways, and my thoughts than your thoughts. For as the rain cometh down, and the snow from heaven, and returneth not thither, but watereth the earth, and maketh it bring forth and bud, that it may give seed to the

> sower, and bread to the eater: So
> shall my word be that goeth forth
> out of my mouth: it shall not
> return unto me void, but it shall
> accomplish that which I please,
> and it shall prosper in the thing
> whereto I sent it. (Isaiah 55:8–11)

We need to clearly understand this and ultimately put our trust in Him. I need to say again, God did not create us to make us happy. God created us to make Him happy. We have a purpose.

We know that God loves us. He loves us so much that He sent His only begotten Son, Jesus Christ, to die on a cross for our sin and pay the price for our sin, and He did that willingly. Jesus rose again from the dead three days after He was crucified to claim victory over sin and spiritual death on our behalf (John 3:16). The love of God is great, powerful, unwavering, and everlasting (Romans 8:31–39).

> He that spared not his own
> Son, but delivered him up for us
> all, how shall he not with him
> also freely give us all things?
> (Romans 8:32)

Here is something to ponder concerning the love of God. We are His creation, and He loves us, right? Satan was also created by God. Do you think that God also loves Satan just as much as He loves us? I do. Even so, Satan will face judgment just as men will. Or I should say that men will face judgment just as Satan will. Jesus died and rose again for all of mankind and gave us hope for eternal life. Satan faces an eternal damnation as prophesied with no hope of redemption (Revelation 20:10). We mankind have hope, and that hope is in God's Son, Jesus Christ alone.

> Jesus saith unto him, I am
> the way, the truth, and the life:
> no man cometh unto the Father,
> but by me. (John 14:6)

Ultimately, all God wants us to do is accept Him and acknowledge who and what He is and love Him in return. To show it—not only in words but in deeds also. To worship Him, and that simply means to be obedient, submitting to His will.

There are some that do not believe in God or Satan and deny their existence. There are some that believe in God but do not believe that Satan exists. Consider this: Without God, there would be no such thing as good, no such thing as morals. Without Satan, there would be no such thing as evil or no such thing as wrongdoing. If neither of them existed, literally any and every act or thought would be okay. We would not have a conscience or any sense of right and wrong.

Right and wrong, or good and evil, as we experience it, is not at all physical. It is our spirit that gives the physical body life that experiences the sense of right and wrong. Our conscience. That conscience is not a physical organ or any type of physical tissue. It is our spirit within the physical body that discerns between right and wrong, good and evil. When your physical body dies, your spirit will not. Your spirit will live eternally. Live where? Heaven or hell, one of the two will be where we all spend eternity. We are in the middle.

> And as it is appointed unto
> men once to die, but after this
> the judgment. (Hebrews 9:27)

WHAT IS OUR PURPOSE?

Knowing that God's way of thinking is above ours and that His ways are not our ways, we naturally still ponder and curiously consider what His purposes for mankind might be. It is only natural that we would like to know and to ask, "Why are we here?"

Throughout Scripture, we can find instructions and guidelines to live by that indicate, guide, and direct us toward our intended purpose. As a Christian who has accepted Jesus, we know that our main purpose is to tell others about Him and be a good witness. We can also find many other lessons throughout Scripture that give us much insight as to what our purpose is.

The story of Job has many lessons for us and is documented in the eighteenth book of the Old Testament. Satan challenges God in Job 1:6–12 and again in Job 2:1–7, and God accepts the challenge from Satan, ultimately granting Satan access to Job and only prohibiting the taking of his life. I often wonder if Satan challenged God during or before His creation of mankind concerning the whole of mankind. Why else would God allow Satan access to Eve in the garden of Eden?

So considering the challenges made by Satan to God concerning Job, we know that God used Job to teach Satan a lesson. There is no doubt in my mind that Satan and his followers challenge God concerning every man, woman, and child on an individual basis. The fact that Satan went to God to present his challenge shows us that God is ultimately in control.

> Be sober, be vigilant;
> because your adversary the devil,
> as a roaring lion, walketh about,
> seeking whom he may devour. (1
> Peter 5:8)

Many people have made the statement that God will not place you under circumstances that you cannot handle. God never said that. It is not indicated in His Word anywhere. What He did say is that He will not allow us to suffer temptation that we cannot bear and that He will give us a way to escape temptation. In other words, He is in control, and He allows us to be tempted by Satan just as He did Eve in the garden of Eden.

> There hath no temptation
> taken you but such as is common
> to man: but God *is* faithful, who
> will not suffer you to be tempted
> above that ye are able; but will

> with the temptation also make
> a way to escape, that ye may be
> able to bear *it*. (1 Corinthians
> 10:13; emphasis mine)

Do you think it is possible that God uses you and me to teach Satan lessons just as He used Job? Do you think it is possible that God is using you and me to teach the angels that fell from heaven and are wandering the earth, attempting to destroy God's creation lessons? They are our adversaries'. We can't see them, but we know they exist, and we know what their intentions and their objectives are. Their main objective is to keep you from God. Remember, it's not all about us; we are in the middle. We ARE the objective.

The spirit warfare exists and originates from the rebellious cherub Lucifer as a self-serving act of defiance toward God. The prizes he fights for are our spirits, intending on keeping you from God and deceiving you into an eternal damnation along with himself and his followers.

Lucifer was created by God for a purpose also. His original purpose was to cover the throne of God. He became proud and arrogant and sinned against God, his creator.

> Thou *art* the anointed
> cherub that covereth; and I have
> set thee *so:* thou wast upon the
> holy mountain of God; thou

hast walked up and down in the midst of the stones of fire. Thou *wast* perfect in thy ways from the day that thou wast created, till iniquity was found in thee. By the multitude of thy merchandise they have filled the midst of thee with violence, and thou hast sinned: therefore I will cast thee as profane out of the mountain of God: and I will destroy thee, O covering cherub, from the midst of the stones of fire. Thine heart was lifted up because of thy beauty, thou hast corrupted thy wisdom by reason of thy brightness: I will cast thee to the ground, I will lay thee before kings, that they may behold thee. Thou hast defiled thy sanctuaries by the multitude of thine iniquities, by the iniquity of thy traffick; therefore will I bring forth a fire from the midst of thee, it shall devour thee, and I will bring thee to ashes upon the earth in the sight of all them that behold thee. All they that know thee among the people shall be astonished at thee: thou shalt be a terror, and never *shalt* thou *be* any more. (Ezekiel 28:14–19; emphasis mine)

Satan doesn't want you to believe in God. Satan doesn't want you to believe that he himself exists. One of the greatest lies he ever told is that Satan does not exist. The last thing he wants is for you to know the truth, and he works tirelessly to keep you from it. But Satan doesn't mind if you believe in God, as long as you do not have a desire to know Him or to have a personal relationship with Him. Satan doesn't mind if you believe in God but do not believe in His Son Jesus. Satan wants you to believe that you are a good person. Satan doesn't mind if you attend church as long as you think that is all you need to do to be in God's favor. Deception is his greatest weapon. Your spirit spending eternity in hell is his main objective.

Because we are in the middle and we are the objective does not mean that we do not have a role or responsibility in the spiritual fight. Nothing is farther from the truth. Satan wants you to believe in destiny, not choice or personal responsibility. We must fight this spiritual battle personally, in spirit, and do it with all commitment.

Many will say that God is on our side. In that context, I disagree. God IS a side. The choice of which side we are on is solely ours, and we are given the free will to choose. We are born with a sin nature and need to change sides. After Satan deceived Eve in the Garden of Eden and Eve chose to sin against God with Adam choosing to make the same decision, we are all born with a sinful, self-centered, self-serving nature as a result.

God wants us to choose Him. Once you choose God and accept Him and God the Son, Jesus Christ, who died for you, then you are on God's side. Once you choose to do that, then God is for you; who can be against you?

> What shall we then say to these things? If God be for us, who can be against us? 32. He that spared not his own Son, but delivered him up for us all, how shall he not with him also freely give us all things? 33. Who shall lay any thing to the charge of God's elect? It is God that justifieth. 34. Who is he that condemneth? It is Christ that died, yea rather, that is risen again, who is even at the right hand of God, who also maketh intercession for us. 35. Who shall separate us from the love of Christ? shall tribulation, or distress, or persecution, or famine, or nakedness, or peril, or sword? 36. As it is written, For thy sake we are killed all the day long; we are accounted as sheep for the slaughter. 37. Nay, in all these

things we are more than con-
querors through him that loved
us. 38. For I am persuaded, that
neither death, nor life, nor angels,
nor principalities, nor powers,
nor things present, nor things to
come, 39. Nor height, nor depth,
nor any other creature, shall be
able to separate us from the love
of God, which is in Christ Jesus
our Lord. (Romans 8:31–39)

GOD CANNOT LIE

Once you choose to be on God's side, there are many wonderful things that occur within you. You are spiritually born again (John 3:3–6). You literally become a child of God, and your spirit is eternally His.

There are many who believe that after you accept Jesus and are on God's side, you can lose that eternal status with Him as being His child. They believe that if you sin again or do something He disapproves of, you lose your status as being His child and are again recondemned to hell. God cannot lie. After you choose to be on His side, He gives your spirit eternal life in heaven with Him after your physical death on earth. Eternal means forever. He will not and cannot go back on His word. He cannot lie. The gift of eternal spiritual life after a physical death is secured eternally and forever through our heartfelt acceptance and belief in His Son Jesus as the only redemption for our sin.

> God is not a man, that he
> should lie; neither the son of
> man, that he should repent: hath
> he said, and shall he not do it? or

hath he spoken, and shall he not make it good? (Numbers 23:19)

In hope of eternal life, which God, that cannot lie, promised before the world began. (Titus 1:2)

That by two immutable things, in which it was impossible for God to lie, we might have a strong consolation, who have fled for refuge to lay hold upon the hope set before us. (Hebrews 6:18)

STRENGTH
THROUGH GOD

How do we fight a determined, unseen adversary? We only have one option. That is through the mighty grace of God. He is the sole provider of spiritual ability that enables us to overcome and have victory over spiritual darkness and spiritual death.

> For we wrestle not against flesh and blood, but against principalities, against powers, against the rulers of the darkness of this world, against spiritual wickedness in high places. (Ephesians 6:12)

Are you even fighting at all? Some aren't even trying and are choosing to willingly live in the spiritual darkness with little or no concern as to what the truth is. If you choose to disregard or deny truth and live in spiritual darkness, then you are willingly subjecting yourself to the rulers of darkness. We need spiritual light to expose them and truth to deny them.

Seemingly limited by our physical five senses and fighting an unseen adversary, are we also limited to fighting blind? Swinging in the dark, so to speak? It seems to some that to fight at all is hopeless, and we are completely defenseless.

Many people are choosing (yes, it is a choice) to fight blind. If we could remove the veil of the flesh—in other words, step out of our body in spirit—then we would see spiritual reality, which is ultimate actual reality, outside and above the physical realm. We are not given that ability, so what are our options to see the spiritual truth and ultimate reality? Only one is available. The light of the world, Jesus Christ the Son of God.

> Then spake Jesus again unto them, saying, I am the light of the world: he that followeth me shall not walk in darkness, but shall have the light of life. (John 8:12)

> Ye are all the children of light, and the children of the day: we are not of the night, nor of darkness. (1 Thessalonians 5:5)

> Jesus saith unto him, I am the way, the truth, and the life: no man cometh unto the Father, but by me. (John 14:6)

We have available to us, all given by God, specific spiritual weapons and defenses described in Ephesians 6:13–17. If we attempt to use these outside of the power of God—in other words, intellectually rather than spiritually—then they just won't work and are not at all effective. A spiritual battle must be fought in spirit and by the spirit. The Word of God, which is the sword of the spirit, cannot be wielded intellectually or physically and be effective. It must be wielded by the spirit or in spirit.

> But the natural man receiveth not the things of the Spirit of God: for they are foolishness unto him: neither can he know them, because they are spiritually discerned. (1 Corinthians 2:14)

To help us better understand these spiritual defenses and weapons, we are given a physical example of an object that we are familiar with to help us relate as to the spiritual applications of them. They are found in Ephesians 6:13–17. To begin with, they are collectively described as "the whole armor of God." Individually, for each piece of the armor, they are described physically as to their intended spiritual effects and purpose, showing us how we should apply them. Our loins girt about with truth and the breastplate of righteousness, our feet shod with the preparation of the gospel of peace, above all the taking shield of faith, the helmet of salvation, and the sword of the spirit, which is the Word of God.

The reason that "above all" is the shield of faith is due to the fact that without faith, you cannot obtain or have any of the others. After this instruction to put on the whole armor of God, we are admonished to communicate and to pray always!

The fact that we are given spiritual armor by God and instructed to put it on shows us again that we have a spiritual purpose, a spiritual responsibility, and an important role in this spirit warfare. The choice is yours: you can put on the whole armor of God spiritually or deny it altogether. Without the armor of God, you are completely defenseless, and to deny it, you are subjecting yourself willingly to your adversary.

> Put on the whole armor of God, that ye may be able to stand against the wiles of the devil. (Ephesians 6:11)

> Wherefore take unto you the whole armor of God, that ye may be able to withstand in the evil day, having done all to stand. (Ephesians 6:13)

Although we are in the middle and we are Satan's objective, it is necessary that we have some objectives of our own. If we lack an objective, then we are simply continually on the defensive, stationary, and never move ahead or make progress of any kind.

Besides guidelines, instructions, and examples to guide and direct us toward our intended purpose, we are also given clear objectives in the Holy Bible. Our ultimate objective is to serve and honor the creator, God the Father, and His Son. How do we do that? We are to learn of Jesus, to be like and live like Jesus, and to tell others about Jesus. Remember, it's not about us. We have a purpose.

To learn of Jesus

> Study to shew thyself approved unto God, a workman that needeth not to be ashamed, rightly dividing the word of truth. (2 Timothy 2:15)

> Take my yoke upon you, and learn of me; for I am meek and lowly in heart: and ye shall find rest unto your souls. (Matthew 11:29)

I have heard many preachers and teachers talk about 2 Timothy 2:15. They all have said that the word *study* in the original Greek text means "to be zealous." That is true if it is used in that context. The Greek word used in 2 Timothy 2:15 is the word *spou-*

dazo. Pronounced, spoo-dad'zo. Guess what? It is also used in the Greek language to mean "STUDY, strive, labor, or endeavor earnestly." Just like some words in the English language, some Greek words can also be used in multiple contexts and have multiple meanings depending on the context of their usage.

Let's break it down and consider the possibilities. In 2 Timothy 2:15, we clearly have an instruction given and also an objective to pursue. The instruction is to "study to show thyself approved unto God." The objective is to be "a workman that needeth not to be ashamed, rightly dividing the word of truth." The objective ultimately describes Jesus Christ Himself. How can we be like Jesus? We need to know Him and study Him so we can be like Him.

You can be zealous to show yourself approved and still not know Jesus. You can be religious and still not know Jesus. We need to study Jesus, and we need to learn of Him to fulfill our purpose and walk in His light to fight this spiritual war and not be subject to the powers of darkness. I believe that when Paul wrote this second letter to Timothy and he said *study*, he meant to learn of, focus on, and study Jesus.

One of the first passages of scripture taught to people around the world is Matthew 11:28–30. Many people have their Sunday school class memorize these verses early on, and especially children. Three little words in verse 29 that are extremely important are often glossed over and receive little, if any, attention: "Learn of me!" Jesus said, "LEARN OF ME. Study Me."

What do you need to do to learn anything? You need to study the subject. Focus on it and study it with the desire of an outcome or end result of complete understanding that you may be productive and accomplish the tasks that require the knowledge gained from studying. Not simply to know, but also to do. How much should we focus on learning about Jesus? He tells us in John 6:50–58.

We all want to be known for something. It is human nature. We desire to be known for something we are good at or where our talents or interests lie. We want to be "that guy" or "that gal." If we ask someone about a problem with our vehicle, we will often receive the advice, "Go to that guy—he eats, sleeps, and breathes Chevy motors." Or if you have a question concerning child behavior, "Go to that gal! She eats, sleeps, and breathes child-rearing and child psychology." What about wanting to be known for being the guy or gal that eats, sleeps, and breathes Jesus? Does God want you to be that guy or that gal? Yes, He does. If someone you don't know approached a coworker of yours and said, "I don't know anything about God, and I wonder if He truly exists or not," would they send them your way saying, "That person eats, sleeps, and breathes Jesus and can answer your questions concerning Him"?

Knowledge is not skill. They are two distinctly separate things. You can have full knowledge and a complete understanding of something and still not be able to perform the necessary tasks and have the skill to complete it.

To actually perform and complete a task satisfactorily, you need to also physically practice it to obtain the skill. For example, you can study the mechanics and science behind hitting a home run with a baseball bat and baseball. You can come to full knowledge and understanding of what it takes, and if you never pick up the bat and put into practice what you have studied, you will never be able to perform the task. To reach our objective and move forward, we also need to, as the old saying goes, practice what we preach.

I believe that Jesus Himself originally coined that phrase. "Eat and drink" is a subject in John 6:50–58. He says, "Eat and drink me." He is not speaking physically but spiritually.

> It is the spirit that quickeneth; the flesh profiteth nothing: the words that I speak unto you, they are spirit, and they are life. (John 6:63)

To be and live like Jesus

As one of our given objectives is to be and live like Jesus, we need to learn to think like Jesus. Seemingly impossible for us to be born with a self-serving, self-centered human nature. It would be impossible if we tried to understand and think like Him in our own intellect.

We need to think like Jesus in spirit. That requires us listening to and submitting to the spirit of God, the Holy Spirit. After we choose God, change sides, and are spiritually reborn, we are given a new influence and priority in spirit and conscience. That higher level of conscience is the influence of the Holy Spirit. Ultimately, it is the Holy Spirit's influence that convinces us to choose God to begin with. We can choose to ignore His influence, being that we still have free will. But to move forward toward our objective of being like and living like Jesus, we must be submissive to the influence of the Holy Spirit and recognize and deny our own sinful humanistic desires.

We need the spiritual light of the Son to move toward our main objective. To be like Jesus, we need to have the mind of Jesus, understanding His objective and adopting His objective as our own. We are to carry on in His work and prioritize His objective as our own. God's spirit, the Holy Spirit, will guide and direct you.

> Forasmuch then as Christ hath suffered for us in the flesh, arm yourselves likewise with the same mind: for he that hath suffered in the flesh hath ceased from sin. (1 Peter 4:1)

> For who hath known the mind of the Lord, that he may

instruct him? But we have the mind of Christ. (1 Corinthians 2:16)

And he said to them all, If any man will come after me, let him deny himself, and take up his cross daily, and follow me. For whosoever will save his life shall lose it: but whosoever will lose his life for my sake, the same shall save it. (Luke 9:23–24)

Then said Jesus unto his disciples, If any man will come after me, let him deny himself, and take up his cross, and follow me. For whosoever will save his life shall lose it: and whosoever will lose his life for my sake shall find it. For what is a man profited, if he shall gain the whole world, and lose his own soul? or what shall a man give in exchange for his soul? For the Son of man shall come in the glory of his Father with his angels; and then he shall reward every man according to his works. (Matthew 16:24–27)

Come unto me, all ye that labour and are heavy laden, and I will give you rest. Take my yoke upon you, and learn of me; for I am meek and lowly in heart: and ye shall find rest unto your souls. For my yoke is easy, and my burden is light. (Matthew 11:28–30)

To witness for Jesus

Jesus not only gave His life on a cross for us, but He spent all of his time, energy, and life on earth witnessing and in service to accomplish His purpose and objective. He was focused. He was serious. He was dedicated to us. Knowing this, we clearly see that we are not only the objective of Satan. We are also the objective of God the Father, God the Son, and God the Holy Spirit. The Holy Trinity.

For God sent not his Son into the world to condemn the world; but that the world through him might be saved. He that believeth on him is not condemned: but he that believeth not is condemned already, because he hath not believed in the name of the only begotten Son of God. And this is the condemnation, that light is come into the world, and men loved darkness rather than light, because their deeds were evil. For every one that doeth evil hateth the light, neither cometh to the light, lest his deeds should be reproved. But he that doeth truth cometh to the light, that his deeds may be manifest, that they are wrought in God. (John 3:17–21)

As we read through Scripture and find the examples, guidelines, and instructions that direct us toward our spiritual purpose, it is obvious that we are to become followers of Jesus and continue working on His behalf to accomplish His objective. His purpose becomes our purpose, and Jesus is the ultimate example.

Obviously, we all cannot dedicate 100 percent of our time and energy to witnessing. We are not all called to be preachers or full-time missionaries, but we are all called to be good witnesses. We have a life given by God, and He placed each of us where He wanted us. We have daily obligations and responsibilities to our family's, employers, and ourselves. During the course of tending to these obligations, we need to be alert and recognize the opportunities to be a witness for Jesus.

There is more than one way to be a good witness. Not everyone is comfortable or confident attempting to verbally present the plan of salvation.

Understand that when it is time, the Holy Spirit will give you the words. The more you talk to people, the easier it becomes. Besides finding the opportunity and talking to people and giving them the truth verbally, we can also simply hand them a tract.

A simple question or comment can open the door to telling someone about Jesus. For example, if you hear someone talking about troubles or concerns, you can ask that individual if they have prayed about them; you can tell them that you will pray for them or even offer to pray with them. These simple comments often open the door to the opportunity to tell them about Jesus. We need to be constantly aware and make an effort to tell people about Jesus. Opportunity should not be passed by. Jesus tells us in Matthew 5:13–16 to let our light shine. We need to be serious. We need to be focused and to be just as dedicated to Jesus as He is to us.

> Ye are the salt of the earth: but if the salt have lost his savour, wherewith shall it be salted? it is thenceforth good for nothing, but to be cast out, and to be trodden under foot of men. Ye are the light of the world. A city that is set on an hill cannot be hid. Neither do men light a candle, and put it under a bushel, but on a candlestick; and it giveth light unto all that are in the house. Let your

light so shine before men, that
they may see your good works,
and glorify your Father which is
in heaven. (Matthew 5:13–16)

THE HOLY
SPIRIT'S WORK

We are to be good witnesses. We are limited to that role. We ourselves cannot convict or convert anyone spiritually, and to attempt to do so is very foolish. That alone is the work of the Holy Spirit. He works in spirit. It is simply our responsibility to present the truth, expose the deception, and be informative, sharing what we know.

Let the Holy Spirit work. Do not attempt to do His work. You may do far more damage than you could ever imagine. Attempting to drive someone or pestering someone into accepting Jesus can easily push them further away from ever knowing and having a personal relationship with God. A good witness will trust the Holy Spirit to do His work.

We have to always keep in the forefront of our minds that it is up to us to listen for Him, to constantly be aware of His instruction and exercise our own free will to be submissive to Him.

But God hath revealed
them unto us by his Spirit: for

the Spirit searcheth all things,
yea, the deep things of God. (1
Corinthians 2:10)

The Holy Spirit is our comforter.

For God hath not given us
the spirit of fear; but of power,
and of love, and of a sound mind.
(2 Timothy 1:7)

Even the Spirit of truth;
whom the world cannot receive,
because it seeth him not, neither
knoweth him: but ye know him;
for he dwelleth with you, and
shall be in you. I will not leave
you comfortless: I will come to
you. (John 14:17–18; emphasis
mine)

The Holy Spirit is our spiritual guide.

Likewise the Spirit also
helpeth our infirmities: for we
know not what we should pray
for as we ought: but the Spirit
itself maketh intercession for us
with groanings which cannot be
uttered. And he that searcheth
the hearts knoweth what is the

mind of the spirit, because he maketh intersession for the saints according to the will of God. (Romans 8:26–27)

Romans 8:1–30 should be studied literally phrase by phrase to better understand the works of the Holy Spirit and what it means to live in spirit.

LESSONS

We spoke about Job earlier and the lessons that the book of Job contains. Many comprehensive books have been written in detail concerning the book of Job, but we are going to look at only a few of the overall details concerning Job and his plight.

Job's faith and dedication to God were the only reasons for the challenges of Satan concerning Job. Remember, Satan doesn't mind at all if you believe there is a God. He just doesn't want you to desire to know Him or have a personal relationship with Him. Job was a righteous and faithful man, dedicated to God. Satan challenged God, and the challenge was that Satan could turn Job away from God. Satan wanted to prove something to God, and Job became his objective. Ultimately, Satan's desire was to hurt God. Job was in the middle.

God accepted Satan's challenge and allowed Satan to attack Job physically, mentally, financially, and spiritually. God granting access to Job shows us that we are also likely used by God to teach Satan lessons. Besides Job being limited by the five physical senses, he also had faith and spiritual strength.

Spiritual ability. God gave Job faith and strength; He did not give him understanding.

Job had no idea about being in the middle and what the actual reality of the situation was. He thought God was angry or displeased with him. That is exactly what Satan wanted him to think, and he wanted Job to lose his faith in God. I firmly believe that if Job knew the full circumstances and that his sufferings were an attack by Satan himself, he would have rejoiced and thanked God for choosing him to represent God and teach Satan a lesson. Satan learned a lesson, lost the challenge, and failed in his attempt to cause Job to turn from God. Our God in us and through us, even as limited as we are, is much stronger and far more powerful than Satan could ever hope to be.

Can we each personally relate to Job and his plight? How often do we have struggles that make us question our faith? How often do we find ourselves asking, "What am I here for? What is my purpose? Why is this happening?" It is critical that we keep in mind the fact that we are in the middle and intentionally not fully informed of the overall plan of God. We are the objective. If we look to and trust in God, He will give us the faith and strength necessary to represent Him in this spiritual war, no matter what the situation or circumstances of them may be. We have an important role, and we have responsibilities.

> Humble yourselves therefore under the mighty hand of

God, that he may exalt you in due time: Casting all your care upon him; for he careth for you. Be sober, be vigilant; because your adversary the devil, as a roaring lion, walketh about, seeking whom he may devour: Whom resist stedfast in the faith, knowing that the same afflictions are accomplished in your brethren that are in the world. But the God of all grace, who hath called us unto his eternal glory by Christ Jesus, after that ye have suffered a while, make you perfect, stablish, strengthen, settle *you*. To him *be* glory and dominion for ever and ever. Amen. (1 Peter 5:6–11; emphasis mine)

Those instructions and guidelines we find throughout Scripture are not always obvious. They can be subtle, and we must have the desire to seek them and recognize them for what they are. It is our responsibility to seek them out and to know them.

To Him *be* glory *and dominion* for ever and ever. Amen.

Who receives the glory in your life? Who have you given your dominion to?

GOD WILL GIVE YOU PEACE

Most people gauge their life, month, or days according to a state of happiness. They understand what being happy is, and they understand sadness. Very few truly understand the state of joy, peace, and contentment. Many people believe that happiness and joy are the same thing. They are not. Happiness is an emotion that can come and go in an instant. Peace, joy, and contentment are states of mind, states of spirit.

> And the peace of God, which passeth all understanding, shall keep your hearts and minds through Christ Jesus. (Philippians 4:7)

> Peace I leave with you, my peace I give unto you: not as the world giveth, give I unto you. Let not your heart be troubled, neither let it be afraid. (John 14:27)

Regardless of your situation, you can be unhappy or sad and at the same time be joyful at peace and content. They are based on spiritual perspective, not emotions. A certain location you know may be peaceful. But it cannot give you spiritual peace. True lasting peace comes from God alone, through the spirit.

THE WILES OF
THE DEVIL

If we are not in service for God and submitting to His will, then we are by default in service for Satan and submitting to his will. Satan wants you in hell. If he can't have you there, he will do everything he can to keep you from a relationship with God, God's will, and serving God. Lucifer had free will to choose to live for his intended purpose and honor his creator, but he chose to rebel and to serve himself. Satan wants you to make the same choice he did.

Our adversaries use lies and deceit. They also use distractions and appeal to your self-serving human nature. They use pride, greed, and arrogance. They use shame. Their goal is to cause you, their objective, to focus on the physical realm and ignore the spiritual. They want you to desire the respected status of men, rather than God. They want you to think that you need to be happy. They simply want to distract you from the spiritual reality and truth.

They do not have the ability to make or force you to turn from or ignore spiritual truth. They attempt to influence and cause you to exercise your own free will to accomplish their goals. They have had around four thousand years of experience to perfect their deceitful tactics. They have been at it since Adam and Eve. They are focused, they are serious, and they are dedicated.

> Beloved, believe not every spirit, but try the spirits whether they are of God: because many false prophets are gone out into the world Hereby know ye the Spirit of God: Every spirit that confesseth that Jesus Christ is come in the flesh is of God: And every spirit that confesseth not that Jesus Christ is come in the flesh is not of God: and this is that *spirit* of antichrist, whereof ye have heard that it should come; and even now already is it in the world. Ye are of God, little children, and have overcome them: because greater is he that is in you, than he that is in the world. (1 John 4:1–4; emphasis mine)

Satan is the father of lies. He will attempt to have you feel hopeful, but it is a false hope. He will attempt to cause you to seek happiness, joy, peace, and contentment in all manner of things that keep your focus away from God. He will appeal to your natural inclinations and instincts to make it happen in the physical realm. Things we can touch and feel, things we can see or hear with no spiritual benefit. Satan will lie to you day in and day out, relentlessly pursuing you, never satisfying and continually leading you to believe that you will be satisfied and fulfilled at some point if you continue to follow his lies.

> Ye are of your father the devil, and the lusts of your father ye will do. He was a murderer from the beginning, and abode not in the truth, because there is no truth in him. When he speaketh a lie, he speaketh of his own: for he is a liar, and the father of it. (John 8:44)

We must be equally determined and relentless in our pursuit of truth—spiritually aware, turning away from anything that is ungodly and serves no legitimate spiritual purpose.

> But be ye doers of the word, and not hearers only, deceiving your own selves. (James 1:22)

There are many who have been deceived into thinking that they can earn a place in heaven through religious works, acts, or deeds. There is no possible way to earn a place in heaven. No matter how religious you are or how hard you work or how zealous and determined you are, it just can't be done.

Satan loves religion. Religion and relationships are not the same thing. Religion is a false comfort, false joy, and false hope. We cannot obtain salvation any way or with any act or effort of our own or through anything other than Jesus. He alone is truth, and accepting Him in spirit is the only way. True Christianity is not a religion. It is a personal relationship with our creator through His Son.

> Jesus saith unto him, I am
> the way, the truth, and the life:
> no man cometh unto the Father,
> but by me. (John 14:6)

> For there is not a just man
> upon earth, that doeth good, and
> sinneth not. (Ecclesiastes 7:20)

Did you know that Satan uses each of us to mock God? Satan is a deceiver, a liar, and he is also an accuser. Even though we are his objective, his purpose is to defy God.

> And I heard a loud voice say
> ing in heaven, Now is come salva
> tion, and strength, and the king
> dom of our God, and the power
> of his Christ: for the accuser of

our brethren is cast down, which accused them before our God day and night. (Revelation 12:10)

COMMANDMENTS

We have seen and discussed a few of the guidelines and instructions given to us in the Scriptures. There are also commandments. The Ten Commandments that Moses was given on Mount Sinai are the most popular and well-known. They were given by God directly to Moses. They are very important to God and should be to us as well.

Jesus was asked specifically in Matthew 22:36, "Which is the great commandment?" In other words, which commandment is the most important? According to Jesus, there is one that is of utmost importance. He said it is the first and great commandment.

> Jesus said unto him, Thou shalt love the Lord thy God with all thy heart, and with all thy soul, and with all thy mind. This is the first and great commandment. And the second *is* like unto it, Thou shalt love thy neighbour as thyself. On these two commandments hang all the law and

the prophets. (Matthew 22:37–
40; emphasis mine)

Disregarding the great commandment and abiding in accordance with all the rest simply makes it religion. Jesus states in Matthew 6:40 that "on these two commandments hang all the law and the prophets," meaning that without abiding by these two, the rest are simply wasted effort on our part and nothing more than an act of religion.

THE WILL OF GOD

We are not clearly given our overall purpose or the overall details of the plan of God. As we read His Word and find the guidelines and instructions given to us, we see very clearly that every one of them guides and directs us to Him, and because of that, we know that we are His objective. We may have questions concerning His ultimate plan and purpose, but we are clearly given what the will of God is for us by Jesus Himself.

The will of God the Father

> And this is the Father's will which hath sent me, that of all which he hath given me I should lose nothing, but should raise it up again at the last day. And this is the will of him that sent me, that every one which seeth the Son, and believeth on him, may have everlasting life: and I will raise him up at the last day. (John 6:39–40)

Draw nigh to God, and He will draw nigh to you. To submit yourself to the will of God and choose Him is a personal choice. We have free will. To do so takes a conscious effort on our part, and we need to be focused, serious, and dedicated. He is for us and desires the same in return. We can deny the will of God as Lucifer did, or we can submit to the will of God and spend eternity with Him, doing our part to fulfill His will. This is done simply by choosing Him and having a desire for a personal relationship with Him on his terms.

> Submit yourselves therefore to God. Resist the devil, and he will flee from you. Draw nigh to God, and he will draw nigh to you. Cleanse *your* hands, *ye* sinners; and purify *your* hearts, *ye* double minded. (James 4:7–8; emphasis mine)

THE GRACE OF GOD

The grace of God is sufficient. It is openly and freely given by Him to anyone who desires to choose Him and receive His spiritual gifts. It is only by the grace of God that we are able to have the light of the Son and be free from the condemnation of sin and spiritual darkness. Only by the grace of God may we spend eternity with Him in heaven. His grace is freely given for us, and it is our choice to accept those spiritual gifts or deny them.

> And he said unto me, My grace is sufficient for thee: for my strength is made perfect in weakness. Most gladly therefore will I rather glory in my infirmities, that the power of Christ may rest upon me. (2 Corinthians 12:9)

> For by grace are ye saved through faith; and that not of yourselves: *it is* the gift of God: Not of works, lest any man

should boast. (Ephesians 2:8–9; emphasis mine)

That if thou shalt confess with thy mouth the Lord Jesus, and shalt believe in thine heart that God hath raised him from the dead, thou shalt be saved. For with the heart man believeth unto righteousness; and with the mouth confession is made unto salvation. For the scripture saith, Whosoever believeth on him shall not be ashamed. For there is no difference between the Jew and the Greek: for the same Lord over all is rich unto all that call upon him. For whosoever shall call upon the name of the Lord shall be saved. (Romans 10:9–13)

Who hath saved us, and called *us* with an holy calling, not according to our works, but according to his own purpose and grace, which was given us in Christ Jesus before the world began, But is now made manifest by the appearing of our Saviour Jesus Christ, who hath abolished death, and hath brought life and immortality to light through the gospel. (2 Timothy 1:9–10; emphasis mine)

God freely gives His grace for our benefit. It is only because God loves us that He gives it to us. The benefits of His grace are spiritual, abundant, and they are eternal. He allows us to be tempted. He allows us to suffer. He allows Satan access to us just as He did with Job, and it is all for the fulfillment of His overall plan, for the fulfillment of His will. We are in the middle. We have a purpose ordained by God and should continually rejoice in His grace regardless of our circumstances.

> But the God of all grace, who hath called us unto his eternal glory by Christ Jesus, after that ye have suffered a while, make you perfect, stablish, strengthen, settle *you*. (1 Peter 5:10; emphasis mine)

> And you hath he quickened, who were dead in trespasses and sins; Wherein in time past ye walked according to the course of this world, according to the prince of the power of the air, the spirit that now worketh in the children of disobedience: Among

whom also we all had our conversation in times past in the lusts of our flesh, fulfilling the desires of the flesh and of the mind; and were by nature the children of wrath, even as others. But God, who is rich in mercy, for his great love wherewith he loved us, Even when we were dead in sins, hath quickened us together with Christ, (by grace ye are saved). (Ephesians 2:1–5)

WORSHIP IN SPIRIT
AND TRUTH

What is worship? If we had to describe it with one single word, that word would simply be *obedience*. Adhering to and following the instructions and guidelines given from the one who gave them with the intentions and purpose of honoring the giver of them rather than yourself. This is not something we should do once a week or now and then on a schedule. True worship is done continuously.

So what does it mean to worship in spirit and truth? It means to have honest spiritual intent. Intent can be easily hidden. The truth can be concealed for a time. Many people go through the motions and appear on the surface to worship but are doing so for reasons other than honoring God. Many attend church regularly with the intent of appearing to worship, having the purpose of being respected for doing so by men—to be accepted among a certain group of friends or for social status. Rather than worship in spirit and truth, they are striving to gain a reputation as a good, upstanding, or righteous person. Be not deceived; God is not mocked. You will reap what you sow.

> Be not deceived; God is not mocked: for whatsoever a man soweth, that shall he also reap. For he that soweth to his flesh shall of the flesh reap corruption; but he that soweth to the Spirit shall of the Spirit reap life everlasting. And let us not be weary in well doing: for in due season we shall reap, if we faint not. (Galatians 6:7–9)

> But he that doeth wrong shall receive for the wrong which he hath done: and there is no respect of persons. (Colossians 3:25)

Only God knows our true intentions. To attempt to worship in words, acts, and deeds but not in spirit is pointless and serves no legitimate purpose in the spiritual realm. Men may be impressed, but God is still waiting for them to turn to Him in spirit and in truth—to choose Him and make Him our priority over earthly or physical desires.

> But the hour cometh, and now is, when the true worship-

pers shall worship the Father in spirit and in truth: for the Father seeketh such to worship him. God *is* a Spirit: and they that worship him must worship *him* in spirit and in truth. (John 4:23–24; emphasis mine)

WALK IN THE SPIRIT

To be obedient and truly worship in spirit, we need to also be walking in the spirit. To do that, we need to be spiritually minded. We need to deny our natural inclinations. If we do not, then there is no possible way to move forward toward our objective, to learn of Jesus, be and live like Jesus, and to witness like Jesus. This means to focus on the spiritual conscience day-to-day, with spiritual awareness and in complete submission to the influence of the Holy Spirit. It takes a conscious effort on our part to do so.

> For though we walk in the flesh, we do not war after the flesh: (For the weapons of our warfare *are* not carnal, but mighty through God to the pulling down of strong holds;) Casting down imaginations, and every high thing that exalteth itself against the knowledge of God, and bringing into captivity every thought to the obedience of Christ; And having in a readiness to revenge

all disobedience, when your obedience is fulfilled. (2 Corinthians 10:3–6; emphasis mine)

Below are a few verses from Galatians chapter 5 and Romans chapter 8. These verses clarify the difference between walking in the flesh versus walking in the spirit. At this point, I would highly recommend that you open your Bible and read the whole chapter of Romans chapter 8.

Spiritual awareness

> *This* I say then, Walk in the Spirit, and ye shall not fulfil the lust of the flesh. For the flesh lusteth against the Spirit, and the Spirit against the flesh: and these are contrary the one to the other: so that ye cannot do the things that ye would. (Galatians 5:16–17; emphasis mine)

> For they that are after the flesh do mind the things of the flesh; but they that are after the Spirit the things of the Spirit. For to be carnally minded *is* death; but to be spiritually minded *is* life and peace. Because the carnal mind *is* enmity against God: for

> it is not subject to the law of God, neither indeed can be. So then they that are in the flesh cannot please God. But ye are not in the flesh, but in the Spirit, if so be that the Spirit of God dwell in you. Now if any man have not the Spirit of Christ, he is none of his. (Romans 8:5–9; emphasis mine)

God provides us with everything we need to walk in the spirit. It is our responsibility to look to Him for everything we need to do so. We do not have the ability to walk in spirit without Him, but we must have the desire for it. If we have the desire, then He gives us everything we need to walk in spirit.

To walk in spirit and make progress toward our objective, we need to have the ability to see the way. As mentioned earlier, we are seemingly limited to only seeing physically, and we need spiritual light to find our way out of spiritual darkness and move forward. The only spiritual light is the Son of God, Jesus. It is His light that gives us hope to make progress and the ability to walk in the spirit. Without Him, we are hopelessly lost.

Using the light of the Son

Jesus is the ultimate example. He is the only begotten Son of God, and He is the light of the world. We see in Hebrews 7:25, Romans 8:34, and 1

John 2:1 that He is not gone but sits at the right hand of the Father, continuing to make intersession for us. He still walks, talks, serves, and lives in spirit, advocating for us to walk, talk, serve, and live as He does.

> Then spake Jesus again
> unto them, saying, I am the light
> of the world: he that followeth
> me shall not walk in darkness,
> but shall have the light of life.
> (John 8:12)

Using the living word of God

The Holy Bible has been described as God's love letter to us. It is that and much more. It is where we look to find our fundamental guidelines, instructions, commandments, faith, and examples to live by. A good way to achieve a fundamental working knowledge of God's Word is to have a consistent method to study it—such as choosing a topic and researching it in the Scriptures. Topics can include love, chastisement, prayer, strength, faith, servitude, relationships, witnessing, distress, and anything else you may have an interest in.

> For the word of God *is*
> quick, and powerful, and sharper
> than any twoedged sword, pierc-
> ing even to the dividing asunder
> of soul and spirit, and of the joints

and marrow, and *is* a discerner of the thoughts and intents of the heart. (Hebrews 4:12; emphasis mine)

Thy word *is* a lamp unto my feet, and a light unto my path. (Psalm 119:105; emphasis mine)

Using prayer

God hears our prayers. He gives us an open, direct line of communication with Him, and He wants us to use it often. We must pray in spirit—simply talking directly to God the Father Himself. It is a personal conversation with our creator. Prayer cannot be a ritualistic saying done intellectually and be effective. Prayer is done in our own words and spirit and with complete honesty. Prayer does not have to be articulated or with complicated verbalization. It must be done in truth and in spirit.

But thou, when thou prayest, enter into thy closet, and when thou hast shut thy door, pray to thy Father which is in secret; and thy Father which seeth in secret shall reward thee openly. But when ye pray, use not vain repetitions, as the heathen *do:* for they think that they shall be heard for their much speaking. Be not ye therefore like unto them: for your Father knoweth what things ye have need of, before ye ask him. (Matthew 6:6–8; emphasis mine)

Let us therefore come boldly unto the throne of grace, that we may obtain mercy, and find grace to help in time of need. (Hebrews 4:16)

But ye, beloved, building up yourselves on your most holy faith, praying in the Holy Ghost, Keep yourselves in the love of God, looking for the mercy of our Lord Jesus Christ unto eternal life. (Jude 1:20–21)

Jesus Himself prayed for you! As we read His words, we realize that His prayer was that the will of God be fulfilled in each of us!

Neither pray I for these alone, but for them also which shall believe on me through their word; That they all may be one; as thou, Father, *art* in me, and I in thee, that they also may be one in us: that the world may believe that thou hast sent me. And the glory which thou gavest me I have given them; that they may be one, even as we are one: I in them, and thou in me, that they may be made perfect in one; and that the world may know that thou hast sent me, and hast loved them, as thou hast loved me. Father, I will that they also, whom thou hast given me, be with me where I am; that they may behold my glory, which thou hast given me: for thou lovedst me before the foundation of the world. (John 17:20–24; emphasis mine)

Communication is extremely important in our spiritual walk. There are many verses of scripture concerning prayer and the importance of it—what it is, what it does for us, and the importance of spending time in prayer.

A few of those verses are listed below:

- Isaiah 65:24
- 1 Peter 3:12
- John 9:31
- Hebrews 4:16

- James 1:6
- Mark 11:24
- Matthew 21:21–22

Using meditation

We are most vulnerable during idle time. To counter that vulnerability, we need to make it a priority to meditate on spiritual matters. To meditate is to ponder or think carefully, deeply, and with focus. Satan wants your thoughts. Obviously, allowing ourselves to spend time to think thoughts that have no spiritual benefit are not spiritually productive.

We all sit and think. We need to prioritize spiritual benefit and productivity over meaningless fantasy. It is our nature to fantasize, and we will all fantasize about all manner of things—a vacation, a lost opportunity, or how we would like to live differently than we are now. To meditate effectively is to mentally consider a certain subject and how it relates to our lives. It takes a focused effort and discipline on our part.

> For though we walk in the flesh, we do not war after the flesh: (For the weapons of our warfare *are* not carnal, but mighty through God to the pulling down of strong holds;) Casting down imaginations, and every high thing that exalteth itself against

the knowledge of God, and bringing into captivity every thought to the obedience of Christ; And having in a readiness to revenge all disobedience, when your obedience is fulfilled. (2 Corinthians 10:3–6; emphasis mine)

I will meditate in thy precepts, and have respect unto thy ways. I will delight myself in thy statutes: I will not forget thy word. (Psalm 119:15–16)

This book of the law shall not depart out of thy mouth; but thou shalt meditate therein day and night, that thou mayest observe to do according to all that is written therein: for then thou shalt make thy way prosperous, and then thou shalt have good success. (Joshua 1:8)

This I say then, Walk in the Spirit, and ye shall not fulfil the lust of the flesh. (Galatians 5:16; emphasis mine)

See then that ye walk circumspectly, not as fools, but

as wise, Redeeming the time, because the days are evil. (Ephesians 5:15–16)

Finally, brethren, whatsoever things are true, whatsoever things *are* honest, whatsoever things *are* just, whatsoever things *are* pure, whatsoever things *are* lovely, whatsoever things *are* of good report; if *there be* any virtue, and if *there be* any praise, think on these things. (Philippians 4:8; emphasis mine)

But put ye on the Lord Jesus Christ, and make not provision for the flesh, to *fulfil* the lusts *thereof.* (Romans 13:14; emphasis mine)

FAITH

Faith is given by God and received by us. Faith must be willingly placed by us and exercised by us. We do not only receive faith from God but must intentionally put our faith in God. When we don't feel like we have faith, we are instructed to put faith in Him. When we have no answers, we still need to remember that we are in the middle. God has a plan and a purpose. Put your faith in God and trust Him; He has all the answers.

Even though we are dealt a measure of faith, we have the gift and responsibility of building on it and increasing our faith through the living word of God.

So then faith cometh by hearing, and hearing by the word of God. (Romans 10:17)

For I say, through the grace given unto me, to every man that is among you, not to think *of himself* more highly than he ought to think; but to think soberly, according as God hath

dealt to every man the measure
of faith. (Romans 12:3; emphasis
mine)

In order to be faithful to our creator and be a faithful follower of His Son, we need to have and put our faith in them. By the grace of God, He has given us the ability to obtain strong faith if we have the desire for it. Read God's Word and trust Him!

THE PLAN OF SALVATION

We are in the middle and must choose a side. It is solely our decision. If you choose to deny God and His Son Jesus, then you have simply made your decision and your choice. It is a choice made in spirit. The life within us that will live eternally after our physical body dies, our spirit, will go into eternity and either reside with God in heaven or will reside in the lake of fire, which is called hell.

> And death and hell were cast into the lake of fire. This is the second death. And whosoever was not found written in the book of life was cast into the lake of fire. (Revelation 20:14–15)

> In flaming fire taking vengeance on them that know not God, and that obey not the gospel of our Lord Jesus Christ: Who shall be punished with

everlasting destruction from the presence of the Lord, and from the glory of his power. (2 Thessalonians 1:8–9)

We are all born in sin, spiritually dead, and headed for an eternity in hell unless we choose God and accept His Son Jesus as our Lord and Savior.

As it is written, There is none righteous, no, not one. (Romans 3:10)

For all have sinned, and come short of the glory of God. (Romans 3:23)

We must be spiritually born again.

Jesus answered and said unto him, Verily, verily, I say unto thee, Except a man be born again, he cannot see the kingdom of God. (John 3:3)

That which is born of the flesh is flesh; and that which is born of the Spirit is spirit. (John 3:6)

Jesus Christ, the Son of God, gave His life on a cross; He was crucified, bled, and died for you and me. The Son of God did that willingly to give us spiritual life and save us from eternal damnation. God loves us!

> For God so loved the world, that he gave his only begotten Son, that whosoever believeth in him should not perish, but have everlasting life For God sent not his Son into the world to condemn the world; but that the world through him might be saved. He that believeth on him is not condemned: but he that believeth not is condemned already, because he hath not believed in the name of the only begotten Son of God. (John 3:16–18)

> But God commendeth his love toward us, in that, while we were yet sinners, Christ died for us. (Romans 5:8)

> Then said Jesus, Father, forgive them; for they know not what they do. And they parted

his raiment, and cast lots. (Luke 23:34)

Accepting the truth, which is Jesus, is the only way. God gave His only Son that we may have salvation from eternal condemnation. It is the gift of God to all men who will accept it.

> For by grace are ye saved through faith; and that not of yourselves: *it is* the gift of God: Not of works, lest any man should boast. (Ephesians 2:8–9; emphasis mine)

> Neither is there salvation in any other: for there is none other name under heaven given among men, whereby we must be saved. (Acts 4:12)

All it takes to receive the gift of salvation from God is faith and acknowledgment to Him. If you know and believe in your heart and in your spirit that Jesus is the Son of God and that He died for you and rose again, then simply talk to Him and tell Him. Admit to Him and confess to Him that you are a sinner and that you believe Jesus died and rose again for you. It is God's gift to us—free, with no effort on our part. It is that simple.

> That if thou shalt confess with thy mouth the Lord Jesus, and shalt believe in thine heart that God hath raised him from the dead, thou shalt be saved. For with the heart man believeth unto righteousness; and with the mouth confession is made unto salvation. (Romans 10:9–10)

SUMMARY

We are the objective. Our spirits, our time, our thoughts, our deeds, and our hearts. We truly are in the middle of spirit warfare. We are in the middle, and there are only two sides to choose from. It is our choice based on our own free will. If you choose to disregard or ignore it, then you are in submission to Satan's will.

Without God's Son, Jesus, His example, and God's Word giving us a working knowledge of the guidelines and instructions given by God, we are fighting blind. Besides the spiritual armor given by God, He also gives us instructions and guidelines on how to use it. We have a responsibility to do so. To seek them and abide in them. Know your adversary and how to fight back. Study Jesus.

First and foremost is to keep our own objective in mind. To be obedient. To be like Jesus, to live like Jesus, and to witness like Jesus. Being serious, focused, and dedicated. If we are, then our idle time will be minimized, and along with it, our vulnerability will be diminished. The more spiritual effort we put into moving toward our objective, the stronger, wiser, and more faithful we become.

> *This* I say then, Walk in the Spirit, and ye shall not fulfil the lust of the flesh. (Galatians 5:16; emphasis mine)

> But in a great house there are not only vessels of gold and of silver, but also of wood and of earth; and some to honour, and some to dishonour. If a man therefore purge himself from these, he shall be a vessel unto honour, sanctified, and meet for the master's use, *and* prepared unto every good work. Flee also youthful lusts: but follow righteousness, faith, charity, peace, with them that call on the Lord out of a pure heart. But foolish and unlearned questions avoid, knowing that they do gender strifes. And the servant of the Lord must not strive; but be gentle unto all *men*, apt to teach, patient, In meekness instructing those that oppose themselves; if God peradventure will give them repentance to the acknowledg-

ing of the truth; And *that* they may recover themselves out of the snare of the devil, who are taken captive by him at his will. (2 Timothy 2:20–26; emphasis mine)

For we have not an high priest which cannot be touched with the feeling of our infirmities; but was in all points tempted like as *we are, yet* without sin. Let us therefore come boldly unto the throne of grace, that we may obtain mercy, and find grace to help in time of need. (Hebrews 4:15–16; emphasis mine)

Submit yourselves therefore to God. Resist the devil, and he will flee from you. Draw nigh to God, and he will draw nigh to you. Cleanse *your* hands, *ye* sinners; and purify *your* hearts, *ye* double minded. Be afflicted, and mourn, and weep: let your laughter be turned to mourning, and *your* joy to heaviness. Humble yourselves in the sight of the Lord, and he shall lift you up. (James 4:7–10; emphasis mine)

Secondly, we must understand their objective. Our adversaries simply want to keep us from God. They cannot force or make you disregard God, so they attempt to deceive you and lure you away from Him with the utmost deception, attempting to cause you to believe any lie they can convince you to believe. They want to accuse you before God, day and night. They want to use you to hurt Him.

> But put ye on the Lord Jesus Christ, and make not provision for the flesh, to *fulfil* the lusts *thereof.* (Romans 13:14; emphasis mine)

> If any of you lack wisdom, let him ask of God, that giveth to all men liberally, and upbraideth not; and it shall be given him. But let him ask in faith, nothing wavering. For he that wavereth is like a wave of the sea driven with the wind and tossed. For let not that man think that he shall receive any thing of the Lord. A double minded man *is* unstable in all his ways. (James 1:5–8; emphasis mine)

You must be spiritually vigilant, exercising awareness, and constantly aware of their attempts to deceive you. They attempt to draw you away subtly, incrementally, little by little. Our adversaries are determined and relentless; we must be also.

> But every man is tempted, when he is drawn away of his own lust, and enticed. Then when lust hath conceived, it bringeth forth sin: and sin, when it is finished, bringeth forth death. Do not err, my beloved brethren. Every good gift and every perfect gift is from above, and cometh down from the Father of lights, with whom is no variableness, neither shadow of turning. Of his own will begat he us with the word of truth, that we should be a kind of firstfruits of his creatures. (James 1:14–18)

Respond to temptation according to God's instruction and guidelines. Our strength and ability to do so come from God alone, and we must respond on His terms, according to His ways—in spirit.

> And have no fellowship with the unfruitful works of darkness, but rather reprove *them*. (Ephesians 5:11; emphasis mine)

Blessed is the man that endureth temptation: for when he is tried, he shall receive the crown of life, which the Lord hath promised to them that love him. Let no man say when he is tempted, I am tempted of God: for God cannot be tempted with evil, neither tempteth he any man: But every man is tempted, when he is drawn away of his own lust, and enticed. Then when lust hath conceived, it bringeth forth sin: and sin, when it is finished, bringeth forth death. Do not err, my beloved brethren. (James 1:12–16)

IT IS NOT GOOD VERSUS EVIL, IT IS EVIL VERSUS GOD.

And ye shall know the truth, and the truth shall make you free. (John 8:32)

For I reckon that the sufferings of this present time are not worthy to be compared with the glory which shall be revealed in us. (Romans 8:18)

It's not all about us. We are in the middle. God has a plan. God has a purpose. He created us for a purpose. Put your faith and trust in Him. Upon our physical death, our spirit will continue to live. Either in heaven or in hell will be where you spend eternity. When your body here on earth dies, you will be, in the beginning.